EXPLORING WORLD CULTURES

Haiti

Joanne Mattern

Cavendish Square

New York

3 9082 14206 5492

Published in 2020 by Cavendish Square Publishing, LLC
243 5th Avenue, Suite 136, New York, NY 10016

Copyright © 2020 by Cavendish Square Publishing, LLC

First Edition

Library of Congress Cataloging-in-Publication Data

Names: Mattern, Joanne, 1963- author.
Title: Haiti / Joanne Mattern.
Description: First edition. | New York : Cavendish Square, [2020] | Series: Exploring world cultures | Includes bibliographical references and index. | Audience: Grades 2-5.
Identifiers: LCCN 2019015211 (print) | LCCN 2019015452 (ebook) | ISBN 9781502651792 (ebook) | ISBN 9781502651785 (library bound) | ISBN 9781502651761 (pbk.) | ISBN 9781502651778 (6 pack)
Subjects: LCSH: Haiti--Juvenile literature.
Classification: LCC F1915.2 (ebook) | LCC F1915.2 .M38 2020 (print) | DDC 972.94--dc23
LC record available at https://lccn.loc.gov/2019015211

Editor: Lauren Miller
Copy Editor: Nathan Heidelberger
Associate Art Director: Alan Sliwinski
Designer: Christina Shults
Production Coordinator: Karol Szymczuk
Photo Research: J8 Media

Printed in the United States of America

Contents

Haiti is a country in the Caribbean Sea. It shares an island with the Dominican Republic. Haiti is a small country. It is filled with mountains and valleys. There are many beautiful beaches too. The people of Haiti are called Haitians.

The island is small, but it is home to millions of people. Many Haitians live in crowded cities. Others live and work on farms in the countryside.

Haiti has an interesting history. Long ago, the country belonged to France. Then, a group of former slaves took over the government. They fought for Haiti to become an independent nation. Since then, Haiti has had many political problems. Much of the nation is very poor.

Despite this, people in Haiti work hard. They

also know how to have fun. Haitians enjoy sports and games. They spend time with family and friends. They share meals and celebrate special holidays together.

Let's learn more about this interesting and beautiful land.

Haitian children play on homemade skateboards. There is not a lot of money for toys, so children make their own.

Haiti is located on the island of Hispaniola. Haiti takes up the western half of the island. The eastern half belongs to a country called the Dominican Republic.

This map shows Haiti's shape and its major cities.

The rest of Haiti is surrounded by water. The Atlantic Ocean lies to the north. The Gulf of Gonâve lies to the west. Gonâve Island is located here. Two **peninsulas**

FACT!

The island of Tortuga lies just off of Haiti's northern coast. Long ago, pirates used to hide on this island.

Hot and Wet Weather

Haiti has a tropical climate. This means the island is very hot and humid. It rains a lot in the spring and fall.

stick out into the sea around the Gulf of Gonâve. To the south is the Caribbean Sea.

In all, Haiti covers 10,714 square miles (27,750 square kilometers). It is about

There are many small islands, like this one, in the Gulf of Gonâve.

55 miles (89 kilometers) from Cuba. A narrow strip of water called the Windward Passage lies between the two countries.

The Taino people lived in Haiti first. Then, in 1492, Christopher Columbus arrived on Hispaniola. He claimed the island for Spain.

Dictator Jean-Claude Duvalier's family ruled Haiti for generations.

In 1697, Spain gave the western part of the island to France. France called its new **colony** Saint-Domingue. Thousands of Africans were sent to Haiti to work as slaves. They grew sugarcane and coffee.

The United States **occupied** Haiti between 1915 and 1934.

8

Haiti is a Taino word that means "land of high mountains." It was the original name for the island of Hispaniola.

In 1791, a former slave named Toussaint Louverture led a **rebellion** against France. Haiti finally became independent in 1804. Jean-Jacques Dessalines became the first ruler of Haiti. He was killed in 1806. This sparked many years of fighting for control of the government.

The Duvalier family ruled Haiti as **dictators** from 1957 to 1986. In 1990, Jean-Bertrand Aristide was elected president by the people. However, things still have not improved politically in Haiti.

VOTE ✓

Haiti wrote a new **constitution** in 1987. It divided the government into three parts. These are the executive, legislative, and judicial branches.

President Jovenel Moïse

The executive branch is led by the president. Haiti's president is elected to a five-year term. He or she cannot serve more than two terms. The executive branch also

FACT!

Haiti has more than fifty recognized political parties.

Going to Court

Most cases in Haiti are decided by a judge. It is hard for people to get a fair trial. This is because poor people cannot afford lawyers.

A Court of Cassation judge reads a decision.

includes the prime minister and a cabinet that advises the prime minister.

The legislative branch is called the National Assembly. It is divided into the Senate and the Chamber of Deputies. Members of the National Assembly make the laws.

The judicial branch runs Haiti's courts. The highest court is the Court of Cassation. It decides how to apply the laws in Haiti.

About 38 percent of Haitians work in farming. They grow rice, corn, yams, mangoes, bananas, and sugarcane. Farmers also raise chickens, goats, and cattle. Most farmers only grow enough food to feed their families.

Farmers use simple tools to plow a field in Haiti.

Some farmers also sell food in markets. Some women bring food and goods from the countryside to sell in the city. They are called the Madan Sara.

FACT!

About 60 percent of Haiti's people live in **poverty**.

Haitian Money

Haitian money is called the gourde. One gourde is worth less than two cents in US money.

Haiti's money celebrates important Haitians.

Some Haitians work in factories. They make clothes, cement, and chemical products. Many factories are owned by companies in the United States.

People from other countries used to visit Haiti, but they stopped because of the political problems. Today, Haiti's government is hoping more tourists will visit. The government is telling people about Haiti's natural beauty and interesting culture.

The Massif du Nord mountain range stretches across Haiti's northern peninsula. The Noires Mountains are located in the middle of the country. The Massif de la Selle mountain

Several mountain ranges divide Haiti.

range is in the south. Between these mountain ranges are flat plains. Many farms are located here.

FACT!

Haiti has more mountains than any other Caribbean nation.

Small and Rare

The Hispaniolan solenodon only lives in Haiti and the Dominican Republic. Its long nose is great for digging up insects and worms.

The Hispaniolan solenodon is a rare poisonous mammal.

Lots of interesting animals live in Haiti. Fish, dolphins, and pilot whales live in the waters around the island. Crabs, mollusks, and sponges live on the coral reefs. On land, frogs and iguanas love Haiti's warm, wet climate. Turtles, snakes, and bats live here too. The nation is also home to about 250 different kinds of birds.

Deforestation is a problem in Haiti. Trees are cut down for farming, building, or firewood.

Almost eleven million people live in Haiti. Most of them are related to the Africans who were brought to Haiti as slaves. In fact, about 95 percent of Haitians have an African background. Other people have

Students in Haiti wear uniforms to school.

ancestors from both Africa and Europe. A small

The average Haitian person only lives to be around sixty-five years old.

Natural Disasters

Haiti often experiences natural disasters. On January 12, 2010, a terrible earthquake struck the country. Many people were killed. Many more lost their homes. It has been difficult to recover from this disaster.

number of Haitians are descended from the original Taino people.

Even though they account for around 5 percent of the population, Haitians with ancestors from both Africa and Europe have controlled most of the nation's wealth and power. On the other hand, the majority of people, mostly black Haitians, are poor. This has caused problems between these two groups.

About half of Haitians live in cities. Port-au-Prince is Haiti's capital and also the largest city. More than one million people live there. Most people in the city live in crowded areas called slums.

Workers painted these houses bright colors after the 2010 earthquake.

In the countryside, the houses are built with wood or clay. The roofs are made of palm leaves

FACT!

The 2010 earthquake destroyed nine out of every ten school buildings in Haiti.

or sheets of tin. These houses often have mud floors and no electricity or running water. Country homes usually have one or two rooms.

Haitian children must go to school from ages six to fifteen. However, many families cannot afford the uniforms, books, or school fees. Few children graduate from school. Rich families often send their children to schools in other countries.

Getting from Here to There

Most roads in Haiti are dirt, and most people do not own a car. In cities, they get around on colorful buses called *tap-taps*.

A colorful *tap-tap* drives through the city streets.

Religion is important to many Haitians. Most Haitians are Christian. Many are a kind of Christian called Roman Catholic. The Spanish brought this religion to Haiti. The French also

A voodoo priest draws a symbol on the ground in cornmeal.

practiced Catholicism when they took over Haiti.

Some people in Haiti are Protestant Christians. People from the United States brought

French law said that all slaves living in French colonies had to be Catholic.

Blessings at the Waterfalls

Every July, Haitians travel to the Saut d'Eau waterfalls to bathe there. This site is very special for both Christians and people who practice voodoo.

People bathe in the Saut d'Eau waterfalls to stay safe in the year ahead.

Protestant beliefs to Haiti about one hundred years ago.

Many Haitians practice a religion called voodoo. African slaves brought voodoo to Haiti. Voodoo says that spirits called *lwa* control the universe. People pray to these spirits for help or blessings. Other nations tried to get rid of voodoo, but it was named one of Haiti's official religions in 2003.

21

Language

One of Haiti's official languages is French. French is used in government and business. It is spoken by rich people too.

A Haitian teacher teaches Creole to her students. Creole is one of Haiti's official languages.

However, most Haitians do not speak French. They speak Haitian Creole (KREE-ole). This language mixes

FACT!

As of 2015, around 61 percent of Haitians could read and write.

The National Anthem

Haiti's national anthem is called "La Dessalinienne." It is named after Jean-Jacques Dessaline, the first ruler of Haiti. This song became the national anthem in 1904.

French and African words. Haitian Creole also includes some Spanish, English, and Taino words.

Today, almost everyone in Haiti speaks Creole. In 1987, the new constitution declared Creole an official language alongside French. Many schools still teach classes in French, however.

People in Haiti's neighbor, the Dominican Republic, speak Spanish. Some Haitians who live along the border also speak some Spanish. Many businesspeople speak English too.

Haitians enjoy art and celebrating. The biggest holiday in Haiti is Carnival. During Carnival, there are parades. People dance, play music, and wear colorful costumes.

Dancers in colorful costumes fill the streets during Carnival.

January 1 is Haiti's Independence Day. Haitians celebrate by

FACT!

Slaves were not allowed to eat the Haitian soup called *joumou*. This is why Haitians eat it today to celebrate their independence.

24

eating a special soup called *joumou*. It is made of squash, potatoes, and meat. April 7 is when Haitians remember Toussaint Louverture, and October 17 celebrates the former ruler Jean-Jacques Dessaline.

The arts are also important. Haitian paintings and sculptures mix African and European culture. The country's most popular music is called *rara*. This music is very lively and includes horns, drums, and bells. Jazz music is also growing in popularity.

Christian Holidays

Haitians celebrate many Christian holidays, including Easter, Corpus Christi, All Saints' Day, and Christmas.

Soccer is the most popular sport in Haiti. People play soccer wherever they can. For example, in cities, they sometimes block off streets to play. Many schools have soccer teams for boys. Haiti also has a professional soccer league with teams all over the country.

Young men enjoy a game of soccer in the street.

Basketball is also a popular sport, especially for girls. People enjoy swimming in the Caribbean

FACT!

Haiti has never won a gold medal in the Summer or Winter Olympics.

26

Tell Me a Story

Haitians love to hear a good story. People often gather around storytellers, who use different voices to tell their tales.

Haitian students listen to their teacher tell a story.

Sea or in the country's rivers. Along the coast, people enjoy fishing, sailing, scuba diving, and more. Games are also very popular. Many Haitians enjoy playing cards or dominoes. They play at home or in the streets.

In voodoo, dancing and drumming are important social activities. People come together to sing and dance during ceremonies.

Many Haitian meals have rice with beans, onions, or peppers. Other vegetables that Haitians like include potatoes, okra, and cabbage. They also eat

A dish of fried plantains makes a tasty meal.

fruits such as avocados, pineapples, and mangoes. Fried plantains are a popular snack.

Most Haitians don't have enough money to buy meat. When they do, they like eating chicken,

FACT!

Crema, or coconut mixed with milk and cinnamon, is a popular drink at Christmas and New Year's.

Yummy Yams

Yams are so popular in Haiti that they have their own holiday. Manger-Yam (Eat Yam) Day happens in November. Of course, people celebrate by eating yams!

Farmers had to dry yams after fields flooded during Hurricane Matthew in 2016.

pork, beef, and goat. People who live near the coast like to eat fish and other seafood.

It is important to have cool drinks in hot weather. *Fresco* is made by pouring syrup from tropical fruits over ice. *Jus papaye* combines papaya juice, milk, sugar, and ice into a drink like a smoothie.

Glossary

colony   An area under the control of another country.

constitution   A document that explains the laws of a country and the rights of the people who live there.

dictators   People who rule a nation by force.

occupied   To be controlled by soldiers from another country.

peninsulas   Land areas surrounded by water on three sides.

poverty   Having so little money that it is a struggle to afford everyday necessities.

rebellion   An act of violence to get rid of a government.

Find Out More

Books

Aronin, Miriam. *Earthquake in Haiti*. New York, NY: Bearport Publishing, 2011.

Bennington, Clara. *Haiti*. Minneapolis, MN: Pogo Books, 2019.

Website

***National Geographic Kids*: Haiti**

kids.nationalgeographic.com/explore/countries/

haiti/#/haiti-girls-running.jpg

Video

A Day in the Life of a Child from Haiti

www.youtube.com/watch?v=wbcDl0iXsug

This video shows a day in the life of a young Haitian girl.

Index

About the Author

Joanne Mattern is the author of more than 250 books for children. She specializes in writing nonfiction and has explored many different places in her writing. Her favorite topics include history, travel, sports, biography, and animals. Mattern lives in New York State with her husband, four children, and several pets.